BinaryCoder X

Building Android App

"Dedicated to the dreamers, the innovators, and the relentless pursuers of excellence in Android app development. May your passion and dedication inspire greatness in all that you create." - BinaryCoder X

"Navigate the boundless realms of creativity, innovation, and possibility in the captivating world of Android app development. With 'Developing Android App' as your guide, the journey to mastery begins here." - BinaryCoder X

Contents

9.

10.

11.

Foreword

In the ever-evolving landscape of technology, few realms hold as much promise and potential for innovation as Android app development. As we stand on the precipice of a new era of mobile experiences, it is my distinct pleasure to introduce you to "Developing Android App" by BinaryCoder X – a comprehensive guide crafted with passion, expertise, and a deep commitment to empowering aspiring developers on their journey to mastery.

In today's digital age, where smartphones have become indispensable extensions of our lives, the role of the Android developer has never been more critical. From revolutionizing industries to shaping the way we communicate, learn, and engage with the world around us, the impact of Android apps is profound and far-reaching.

Drawing upon my own experiences navigating the ever-shifting currents of the app development landscape, I've endeavored to distill the essence of Android app development into a single, comprehensive resource that empowers developers of all levels to unleash their creativity and bring their ideas to life.

Within the pages of this book, you'll find a treasure trove of knowledge, insights, and practical advice that will guide you through every stage of the development process – from conceptualization and design to coding, testing, and beyond. Whether you're a seasoned professional looking to sharpen your skills or a novice eager to embark on your coding journey, this book has something for everyone.

But beyond the technical aspects of development, "Developing Android App" is also a testament to the spirit of innovation, collaboration, and community that defines the Android ecosystem. It is a celebration of the countless developers, designers, and enthusiasts who, through their passion and dedication, have helped shape the Android platform into what it is today.

As you embark on this journey, remember that the path to mastery is not always easy, but it is always rewarding. Embrace the challenges, savor the victories, and never lose sight of the incredible potential that lies within your grasp.

With "Developing Android App" as your guide, I invite you to embark on a journey of discovery, exploration, and boundless creativity. Together, let us push the boundaries of what's possible and unlock the full potential of Android app development.

Happy coding!

BinaryCoder   X

Preface

Preface:

Welcome to the captivating world of Android app development, where imagination meets innovation, and possibilities abound. In this dynamic realm, BinaryCoder X invites you on an exhilarating journey to unlock the secrets of crafting immersive, feature-rich Android applications that captivate audiences and transform ideas into reality.

With the rapid proliferation of mobile technology, the demand for exceptional Android experiences has never been greater. As the landscape continues to evolve, developers must rise to the challenge, armed with the knowledge, skills, and creativity to create apps that leave a lasting impression.

In this comprehensive guide, BinaryCoder X draws upon years of experience and expertise to provide aspiring developers with a roadmap to success. From the initial stages of conceptualization and design to the intricacies of coding and optimization, each chapter offers invaluable insights and practical guidance to navigate the complexities of Android app development with confidence and proficiency.

Whether you're a seasoned developer seeking to expand your repertoire or a newcomer eager to embark on your coding odyssey, this book serves as your indispensable companion on the path to mastery. Through hands-on tutorials, real-world examples, and expert advice, you'll learn not only the technical intricacies of Android development but also the art of crafting compelling user experiences that resonate with audiences worldwide.

So, dear reader, prepare to embark on a thrilling adventure into the heart of Android app development. With BinaryCoder X as your guide, the possibilities are limitless, and the journey promises to be nothing short of extraordinary. Let's dive in and unleash the power of imagination, innovation, and ingenuity to create the next generation of Android masterpieces.

Acknowledgement

Acknowledgements:

As I stand on the threshold of introducing "Developing Android App" to the world, I am filled with profound gratitude for the countless individuals whose support, guidance, and inspiration have made this endeavor possible.

First and foremost, I would like to express my heartfelt appreciation to my family and friends for their unwavering encouragement and belief in my abilities. Their steadfast support has been a source of strength and motivation throughout this journey, and I am endlessly grateful for their love and encouragement.

I extend my deepest gratitude to the team at BinaryCoder Publishing for their dedication and commitment to excellence in bringing this book to fruition. Their expertise, professionalism, and passion for the craft of publishing have been instrumental in shaping this project into a reality.

I am indebted to the countless mentors, colleagues, and industry experts who have generously shared their knowledge, insights, and expertise with me over the years. Their guidance has been invaluable in shaping my understanding of Android app development and pushing the boundaries of my own capabilities.

I would also like to thank the vibrant Android developer community for their camaraderie, collaboration, and spirit of innovation. The exchange of ideas, the camaraderie, and the collective pursuit of excellence have enriched my own journey as a developer and inspired me to strive for greatness.

Last but certainly not least, I am profoundly grateful to the readers of "Developing Android App" for their interest, enthusiasm, and curiosity. It is my sincere hope that this book serves as a valuable resource and companion on your own journey of Android app development, empowering you to unlock your full potential and make a meaningful impact in the world.

In closing, I extend my deepest appreciation to all who have contributed to the creation of this book. Your support and encouragement have been the driving force behind its creation, and for that, I am eternally grateful.

With heartfelt thanks,

BinaryCoder   X

1

Define Your Idea

Defining your app idea involves clearly outlining its purpose, features, target audience, and potential value proposition. Here are a few examples to illustrate:

1. **Fitness Tracker App**:
   - Idea: Develop an app that helps users track their fitness activities, such as running, cycling, and gym workouts.
   - Features: GPS tracking, workout logging, calorie tracking, goal setting, progress charts, social sharing.
   - Target Audience: Fitness enthusiasts, athletes, people looking to improve their health and wellness.
   - Value Proposition: Provides users with a convenient and comprehensive tool to monitor and improve their fitness levels.

2. **Language Learning App**:

   - Idea: Create an app that facilitates language learning through interactive lessons, quizzes, and cultural insights.

   - Features: Vocabulary lessons, grammar exercises, pronunciation practice, real-life dialogues, progress tracking.

   - Target Audience: Students, professionals, travelers, anyone interested in learning a new language.

   - Value Proposition: Offers an engaging and effective way for users to acquire language skills at their own pace and convenience.

3. **Recipe Sharing App**:

   - Idea: Build a platform where users can discover, share, and save recipes from various cuisines and dietary preferences.

   - Features: Recipe search, ingredient list, cooking instructions, user profiles, rating and reviews, meal planning.

   - Target Audience: Home cooks, foodies, people with dietary restrictions or special dietary preferences.

   - Value Proposition: Enables users to explore a wide range of recipes, connect with a community of fellow food enthusiasts, and find inspiration for their culinary adventures.

4. **Task Management App**:

   - Idea: Develop an app to help individuals and teams organize tasks, prioritize work, and collaborate effectively.

- Features: Task lists, due dates, reminders, task assignment, progress tracking, file attachments, team chat.

- Target Audience: Students, professionals, project managers, freelancers, small businesses.

- Value Proposition: Streamlines task management processes, improves productivity, and fosters better communication and collaboration among users.

These examples demonstrate the importance of clearly defining the purpose, features, target audience, and value proposition of your app before diving into development. This clarity helps guide the development process and ensures that your app addresses real user needs and provides meaningful value.

Certainly, continuing from where we left off:

5. **E-commerce App**:
- Idea: Create a mobile platform for buying and selling products across various categories.

- Features: Product listings, search and filter options, user profiles, shopping cart, secure checkout, order tracking, ratings and reviews.

- Target Audience: Online shoppers, retailers, small businesses, anyone looking to buy or sell products online.

- Value Proposition: Offers a convenient and accessible marketplace for users to discover, purchase, and sell goods, along with features like personalized recommendations and secure transactions.

6. **Travel Planning App**:

   - Idea: Develop an app to assist users in planning and organizing their travel itineraries.

   - Features: Destination guides, flight and hotel bookings, itinerary creation, travel expense tracking, local recommendations, trip sharing.

   - Target Audience: Travel enthusiasts, vacationers, business travelers, adventure seekers.

   - Value Proposition: Helps users streamline the travel planning process, discover new destinations, and make the most out of their travel experiences with personalized recommendations and convenient booking options.

7. **Mental Health App**:

   - Idea: Build an app to support mental health and well-being through meditation, mindfulness, and therapy resources.

   - Features: Guided meditation sessions, mood tracking, journaling, coping strategies, therapist directories, community support.

- Target Audience: Individuals dealing with stress, anxiety, depression, or seeking to improve their overall mental wellness.

- Value Proposition: Provides users with accessible tools and resources to manage their mental health, build resilience, and connect with supportive communities, promoting overall well-being and self-care.

8. **Home Automation App**:

- Idea: Develop an app to control smart home devices, such as lights, thermostats, cameras, and appliances.

- Features: Device control, scheduling, automation routines, energy monitoring, notifications, remote access.

- Target Audience: Homeowners, tech enthusiasts, anyone interested in enhancing home convenience and efficiency.

- Value Proposition: Offers users the ability to manage and automate their home environment, improving comfort, security, and energy efficiency through seamless integration and control of smart devices.

These examples showcase a diverse range of app ideas, each with its unique purpose, features, target audience, and value proposition. By carefully defining your app idea in this manner, you can better conceptualize and communicate your vision, laying the foundation for successful development and user adoption.

Certainly, here are a few more examples:

9. **Study Aid App**:

   - Idea: Create an app to assist students in their studies by providing access to educational resources, study tools, and collaborative learning features.

   - Features: Flashcards, quizzes, study guides, note-taking, group study sessions, textbook access, progress tracking.

   - Target Audience: Students of all ages, educators, lifelong learners.

   - Value Proposition: Offers a comprehensive platform for academic support, helping users enhance their learning experience, improve retention, and achieve academic success through interactive study materials and peer collaboration.

10. **Event Planning App**:

   - Idea: Develop an app to streamline event planning processes, from invitations and RSVPs to venue selection and coordination.

   - Features: Event creation, guest lists, invitations, RSVP management, budget tracking, vendor contacts, task assignments.

- Target Audience: Event planners, party hosts, organizations, businesses.

- Value Proposition: Simplifies event management tasks, saves time and effort for organizers, and ensures seamless coordination and communication among all stakeholders involved in planning and executing events.

11. **Personal Finance App**:

- Idea: Build an app to help users manage their finances, track expenses, set budgets, and achieve financial goals.

- Features: Expense tracking, budgeting tools, bill reminders, savings goals, investment portfolio tracking, financial insights.

- Target Audience: Individuals seeking to improve their financial health, budget-conscious consumers, investors.

- Value Proposition: Empowers users to take control of their finances, make informed financial decisions, and work towards achieving their short-term and long-term financial objectives through effective budgeting and money management tools.

12. **Pet Care App**:

- Idea: Create an app to assist pet owners in managing their pets' health, nutrition, and daily care routines.

- Features: Pet profiles, vaccination reminders, grooming schedules, pet food recommendations, vet locator, community forums.

- Target Audience: Pet owners, animal lovers, veterinarians, pet care professionals.

- Value Proposition: Provides a centralized platform for pet care management, helping users ensure the well-being of their furry companions, stay organized with pet-related tasks, and connect with a community of fellow pet owners for advice and support.

These additional examples highlight the diverse possibilities for app development, catering to various interests, needs, and industries. By defining your app idea with clarity and purpose, you can create a compelling product that resonates with your target audience and delivers tangible value.

Of course, here are a few more examples:

13. **Music Streaming App**:
- Idea: Develop an app for streaming and discovering music from a vast library of songs, albums, and playlists.

- Features: Personalized recommendations, curated playlists, offline listening, social sharing, artist profiles, lyric display.

- Target Audience: Music enthusiasts, casual listeners, audiophiles, anyone who enjoys exploring new music.

- Value Proposition: Offers a convenient and immersive music listening experience, tailored to individual preferences, with access to a diverse range of music content and discovery tools.

14. **Remote Work Collaboration App**:

- Idea: Create an app to facilitate remote team collaboration, communication, and project management.

- Features: Chat messaging, video conferencing, file sharing, task boards, calendar integration, virtual meetings.

- Target Audience: Remote workers, distributed teams, freelancers, businesses embracing remote work.

- Value Proposition: Enhances productivity and teamwork among remote workers, enabling seamless communication, collaboration, and project coordination across different locations and time zones.

15. **Photo Editing and Sharing App**:

- Idea: Build an app for editing, enhancing, and sharing photos with friends and followers.

- Features: Filters and effects, cropping and resizing tools, photo adjustments, social media integration, photo tagging.

- Target Audience: Photography enthusiasts, social media users, content creators.

- Value Proposition: Empowers users to express their creativity, beautify their photos, and share memorable moments with others through a user-friendly and feature-rich photo editing and sharing platform.

16. **Language Translation App**:

- Idea: Develop an app for translating text and speech between different languages in real-time.

- Features: Text translation, speech-to-text and text-to-speech conversion, language detection, offline mode, conversation mode.

- Target Audience: Travelers, international business professionals, language learners, individuals interacting with multilingual communities.

- Value Proposition: Breaks down language barriers and facilitates communication across diverse linguistic backgrounds, making it easier for users to connect, interact, and navigate in a globalized world.

These examples illustrate the wide range of possibilities for app development, catering to various interests, needs, and industries. Whether it's entertainment, productivity, communication, or utility, defining your app idea with clarity and purpose is essential for creating a compelling and successful   product.

2

Learn The Basics

Learning the basics of Android app development involves understanding fundamental concepts, tools, and programming languages. Here's an explanation with examples:

1. **Programming Languages**:
   - **Java**: Java is the traditional language for Android development. It's widely used and supported, making it a good choice for beginners. Example:

```java
public class MainActivity extends AppCompatActivity {
@Override
protected void onCreate(Bundle savedInstanceState) {
super.onCreate(savedInstanceState);
setContentView(R.layout.activity_main);
}
}
```

```
- **Kotlin**: Kotlin is a modern programming language that offers concise syntax and enhanced features compared to Java. It's officially supported by Google for Android development. Example:
```kotlin
class MainActivity : AppCompatActivity() {
override fun onCreate(savedInstanceState: Bundle?) {
super.onCreate(savedInstanceState)
setContentView(R.layout.activity_main)
}
}
```

2. **XML for Layout Design**:

- XML (eXtensible Markup Language) is used to create layout designs for Android app screens. It defines the structure and appearance of UI elements. Example:
```xml
<?xml version="1.0" encoding="utf-8"?>
<RelativeLayout
xmlns:android="http://schemas.android.com/apk/res/android"

android:layout_width="match_parent"
android:layout_height="match_parent">
```
```

```
<TextView
    android:id="@+id/textView"
    android:layout_width="wrap_content"
    android:layout_height="wrap_content"
    android:text="Hello, World!"
    android:layout_centerInParent="true"/>

</RelativeLayout>
```

3. **Android Studio**:

   - Android Studio is the official Integrated Development Environment (IDE) for Android development. It provides a comprehensive set of tools for building, debugging, and testing Android apps. Example:

`![Android Studio Example](https://developer.android.com/studio/images/studio-icon-preview.svg)`

4. **Understanding Activity Lifecycle**:

   - Activities in Android have a lifecycle, consisting of various states such as onCreate, onStart, onResume, onPause, onStop, and onDestroy. Understanding this lifecycle is crucial for managing app behavior and resources efficiently. Example:

```java
public class MainActivity extends AppCompatActivity {
@Override
protected void onCreate(Bundle savedInstanceState) {
super.onCreate(savedInstanceState);
setContentView(R.layout.activity_main);

}


@Override
protected void onResume() {
super.onResume();
// Code to resume any paused functionality

}
}
```

5. **Using Intents for Navigation**:
   - Intents are used for communication between components in an Android app, such as starting activities, sending broadcasts, and invoking services. Example:

```java
Intent intent = new Intent(MainActivity.this, SecondActivity.class);
startActivity(intent);
```

These basics provide a solid foundation for getting started with Android app development. As you progress, you'll delve deeper into more advanced topics and techniques to build robust and feature-rich applications.

6. **User Interface (UI) Components**:

- Android provides a rich set of UI components to create interactive and visually appealing interfaces. Some common UI components include TextView, Button, EditText, RecyclerView, and ImageView. Example:

```xml
<Button
android:id="@+id/button"
android:layout_width="wrap_content"
android:layout_height="wrap_content"
android:text="Click Me"
android:onClick="onClick"/>
```


7. **Handling User Input**:

- Android apps often require user input for various purposes, such as form submission, search queries, or interacting with elements. Handling user input involves capturing and processing data entered by the user. Example:
```java
```

```java
Button button = findViewById(R.id.button);
button.setOnClickListener(new    View.OnClickListener()
{

@Override
public void onClick(View v) {
// Handle button click event
}
});
```

8. **Data Storage**:

   - Android apps may need to store data locally on the device for offline access or to maintain user preferences. Common options for data storage include SharedPreferences for simple key-value pairs, SQLite database for structured data, and files for storing larger datasets. Example:

```java
SharedPreferences          preferences          =
getSharedPreferences("MyPrefs",
Context.MODE_PRIVATE);
SharedPreferences.Editor editor = preferences.edit();
editor.putString("username", "JohnDoe");
editor.apply();
```

9. **Networking**:

   - Many Android apps interact with remote servers to fetch data, upload files, or communicate with web services. Android provides classes like HttpURLConnection, OkHttp, and Retrofit to handle network requests. Example using Retrofit for making HTTP requests:

```java
Retrofit retrofit = new Retrofit.Builder()
.baseUrl("https://api.example.com/")
.addConverterFactory(GsonConverterFactory.create())
.build();
MyApiService service = retrofit.create(MyApiService.class);
Call<User> call = service.getUser(userId);
```

10. **Permissions**:

   - Android apps require permissions to access certain device features or data, such as camera, location, storage, etc. Requesting permissions from the user is essential for ensuring app functionality and security. Example:

```java
if (ContextCompat.checkSelfPermission(MainActivity.this, Manifest.permission.ACCESS_FINE_LOCATION)
!= PackageManager.PERMISSION_GRANTED) {
```

ActivityCompat.requestPermissions(MainActivity.this,
new
String[]{Manifest.permission.ACCESS_FINE_LOCATION}
, REQUEST_LOCATION_PERMISSION);
    }
    ```

These additional concepts are essential for building dynamic, functional, and user-friendly Android applications. Mastering them will enable you to create versatile apps that meet the needs and expectations of your users.

Certainly! Let's continue with a few more fundamental concepts:

11. **Handling App Resources**:
    - Android apps utilize various types of resources such as images, strings, colors, and layouts. Managing these resources efficiently is crucial for maintaining a clean and organized codebase. Example of accessing a string resource in XML:
    ```xml
    <TextView
    android:layout_width="wrap_content"
    android:layout_height="wrap_content"
```
```

android:text=”@string/welcome_message” />
```

12. **Adapting to Different Screen Sizes and Orientations**:
   - Android devices come in various screen sizes and orientations, so your app needs to adapt its layout and design accordingly. Concepts like responsive design, layout constraints, and alternative resources (e.g., different layout files for landscape and portrait modes) help ensure a consistent user experience across devices. Example of using layout constraints in XML:
   ```xml
   <TextView
   android:id=”@+id/textView”
   android:layout_width=“wrap_content”
   android:layout_height=“wrap_content”
   app:layout_constraintTop_toTopOf=“parent”
   app:layout_constraintStart_toStartOf=“parent”
   app:layout_constraintEnd_toEndOf=“parent”
   app:layout_constraintBottom_toBottomOf=“parent”
   android:text=“Centered Text” />
   ```

13. **Debugging and Logging**:
   - Debugging is an essential skill for troubleshooting issues and improving the quality of your app. Android
   ```

provides tools like Logcat for viewing log messages and debugging information. Logging statements help you track the flow of your app and identify potential bugs. Example of logging a message in Java:

```java
Log.d("MainActivity", "Button clicked");
```


14. **Version Control**:

   - Version control systems like Git help you manage changes to your codebase, collaborate with other developers, and track the history of your project. Platforms like GitHub, GitLab, and Bitbucket provide hosting services for Git repositories. Example of basic Git commands:

```
git init
git add .
git commit -m "Initial commit"
git remote add origin <repository_url>
git push -u origin master
```


15. **Continuous Integration and Deployment (CI/CD)**:

   - CI/CD practices automate the process of building, testing, and deploying your app, allowing for faster iteration and delivery. Tools like Jenkins, Travis CI, and CircleCI help

automate these workflows, ensuring code quality and reliability. Example of a CI/CD pipeline:
```

Build -> Test -> Analyze -> Package -> Deploy
```


These additional concepts complement your understanding of Android app development and contribute to building robust, scalable, and maintainable applications. Continuously learning and mastering these skills will empower you to create high-quality apps that meet user expectations and industry standards.

Certainly! Let's explore a few more essential concepts:

16. **Error Handling**:
   - Error handling is crucial for ensuring that your app behaves gracefully in unexpected situations. Properly handling errors prevents crashes and enhances the user experience. Techniques include using try-catch blocks, handling exceptions, and displaying informative error messages. Example of error handling in Java:
```java
try {
// Code that may throw an exception
```

```
} catch (Exception e) {
// Handle the exception
Log.e("MainActivity", "An error occurred: " + e.getMessage());
    }
```

17. **Localization and Internationalization**:

- To reach a global audience, your app should support multiple languages and cultural preferences. Localization involves translating your app's content and adapting it to different regions, while internationalization ensures that your app is designed to handle various languages and formats. Example of localizing a string resource in multiple languages:
```

values/strings.xml (English)
```
<string name="welcome_message">Welcome to the App!</string>
```

values-fr/strings.xml (French)
```
<string name="welcome_message">Bienvenue dans l'application !</string>
```
```

18. **Security Best Practices**:

- Security is paramount in app development to protect user data and privacy. Implementing measures such as secure network communication (HTTPS), data encryption, user authentication, and secure storage help safeguard your app against various threats and vulnerabilities. Example of encrypting sensitive data:

```java
String encryptedData = encryptData(sensitiveData);
```


19. **Performance Optimization**:

- Optimizing your app's performance ensures smooth and responsive user experiences. Techniques include minimizing memory usage, optimizing UI rendering, reducing network calls, implementing caching mechanisms, and profiling your app for performance bottlenecks. Example of optimizing image loading with Glide library:

```java
Glide.with(context)
.load(imageUrl)
.into(imageView);
```

20. **User Feedback and Analytics**:

   - Gathering feedback from users and analyzing app usage metrics are essential for improving your app over time. Integrating features like in-app feedback forms, user surveys, crash reporting, and analytics tools (e.g., Google Analytics, Firebase Analytics) provides valuable insights into user behavior and preferences. Example of tracking a user event with Firebase Analytics:
   ```java
   Bundle params = new Bundle();
   params.putString("button_clicked", "home_screen");
   firebaseAnalytics.logEvent("button_click", params);
   ```


By understanding and applying these advanced concepts, you'll be able to create high-quality Android apps that meet user expectations for functionality, security, performance, and usability. Continuing to learn and adapt to emerging trends and technologies will further enhance your skills as an Android   developer.

3

Set-up Developing Environment

Setting up your development environment for Android app development involves installing the necessary tools and configuring them to work together seamlessly. Here's a step-by-step guide with examples:

1. **Install Java Development Kit (JDK)**:
   - Download and install the JDK from the official Oracle website or use a package manager like Homebrew on macOS.

   - Example of installing JDK using Homebrew on macOS:
   ```

   brew install —cask adoptopenjdk
   ```

2. **Install Android Studio**:

- Android Studio is the official IDE for Android development, providing a comprehensive set of tools for building Android apps.

- Download and install Android Studio from the official website.

- Example of installing Android Studio on macOS using Homebrew Cask:

```
brew install —cask android-studio
```

3. **Set up Android SDK**:

- Android Studio includes the Android SDK (Software Development Kit), which contains necessary tools, libraries, and system images for building Android apps.

- During the Android Studio installation process, ensure that the required SDK components are downloaded and installed.

- You can also manage SDK components using the SDK Manager within Android Studio.

4. **Configure Android Virtual Device (AVD)**:

- AVD allows you to emulate Android devices on your development machine for testing and debugging.

- Open Android Studio, navigate to Tools > AVD Manager, and create a new virtual device.

- Choose a device definition (e.g., Pixel), select a system image (e.g., Android API level), and configure additional settings as needed.

5. **Install Android SDK Tools and Build Dependencies**:

- Android SDK tools and build dependencies are required for compiling, building, and deploying Android apps.

- Ensure that the necessary SDK tools and build dependencies are installed through the SDK Manager in Android Studio.

6. **Set up Device for USB Debugging**:

- If you prefer testing your app on physical devices, enable USB debugging on your Android device.

- Go to Settings > Developer options (enable Developer options if not already enabled) > USB debugging, and toggle the switch to enable it.

- Connect your device to your development machine via USB cable.

7. **Create a New Project in Android Studio**:

- Open Android Studio and select "Start a new Android Studio project."

- Follow the project creation wizard to configure your project settings, including project name, package name, target SDK version, and minimum SDK version.

8. **Verify Setup**:

   - Once your project is created, ensure that you can build and run it on either the Android Emulator or a physical device connected to your development machine.

   - Run the app by clicking the "Run" button in Android Studio or selecting "Run" from the Run menu.

By following these steps, you'll have set up a fully functional development environment for Android app development using Android Studio. You can now start coding and building your Android apps with ease.

9. **Import Additional Dependencies (Optional)**:

   - Depending on the requirements of your project, you may need to import additional libraries or dependencies to enhance functionality or streamline development.

   - Add dependencies to your project's build.gradle file, either at the module level (app-level) or the project level. Example of adding a dependency for Retrofit, a popular HTTP client library, in the app-level build.gradle file:

```groovy
```

```
dependencies {
implementation 'com.squareup.retrofit2:retrofit:2.9.0'
implementation             'com.squareup.retrofit2:converter-
gson:2.9.0'
}
```

10. **Configure Version Control (Optional)**:

- If you plan to use version control for managing your project's source code, set up Git integration within Android Studio.

- Initialize a new Git repository for your project or clone an existing repository from a remote Git server (e.g., GitHub, GitLab).

- Configure Git settings, such as username and email address, within Android Studio's version control settings.

11. **Explore Documentation and Resources**:

- Familiarize yourself with the official Android documentation, developer guides, and API references provided by Google.

- Utilize online resources, forums, and communities such as Stack Overflow, Reddit, and the Android Developers community for troubleshooting issues, seeking advice, and staying updated on best practices and industry trends.

12. **Set Up Emulator Acceleration (Optional)**:

   - To improve the performance of the Android Emulator, consider enabling hardware acceleration (HAXM or Intel HAXM on Intel-based systems, or Hyper-V on AMD-based systems) if your development machine supports it.

   - Configure virtualization settings in your computer's BIOS or UEFI firmware and install the appropriate virtualization software.

13. **Explore Android Studio Features**:

   - Take some time to explore the features and capabilities of Android Studio, including code editing tools, debugging utilities, layout editors, and performance profiling tools.

   - Familiarize yourself with keyboard shortcuts and productivity-enhancing features to streamline your development workflow.

14. **Stay Updated and Experiment**:

   - Android development is a dynamic field with frequent updates and new features. Stay updated with the latest releases, tools, and practices to keep your skills relevant.

   - Experiment with different app ideas, techniques, and frameworks to broaden your knowledge and deepen your understanding of Android development.

By following these additional steps and tips, you'll be well-equipped to leverage the full potential of Android Studio and build high-quality Android apps efficiently. Happy coding!

15. **Test Your App on Various Devices and Android Versions**:

- While developing your app, it's essential to test it on a variety of devices and Android versions to ensure compatibility and optimal performance across different configurations.

- Use the Android Emulator to test your app on various virtual devices with different screen sizes, resolutions, and hardware configurations.

- If possible, test your app on physical devices representing different manufacturers, screen sizes, and Android versions to identify and address any device-specific issues.

16. **Optimize Your Development Workflow**:

- Streamline your development workflow by leveraging Android Studio's features such as code templates, live templates, code completion, and refactoring tools.

- Configure keyboard shortcuts and customizations to suit your preferences and improve productivity.

- Consider using productivity plugins and extensions available for Android Studio to automate repetitive tasks and enhance your development experience.

17. **Utilize Debugging and Profiling Tools**:

- Android Studio provides powerful debugging and profiling tools to help you identify and resolve issues in your app.

- Use the debugger to step through your code, inspect variables, and diagnose runtime errors.

- Utilize the Android Profiler to analyze your app's CPU, memory, and network usage, identify performance bottlenecks, and optimize your app for efficiency.

18. **Stay Informed About Platform Changes and Best Practices**:

- Stay updated with the latest developments in the Android platform, including new features, APIs, and best practices.

- Attend Android developer conferences, webinars, and meetups to learn from industry experts, network with fellow developers, and stay informed about emerging trends and technologies.

- Follow reputable Android development blogs, forums, and social media channels to receive timely updates, tips, and tutorials.

19. **Seek Feedback and Iterate**:

- Solicit feedback from users, colleagues, and beta testers to gather insights into your app's usability, performance, and user experience.

- Act on feedback by iterating on your app's design, functionality, and features to address user needs and preferences.

- Embrace an iterative development process, continuously improving and refining your app based on user feedback and data-driven insights.

20. **Publish Your App to the Google Play Store**:

- Once your app is ready for release, prepare it for deployment to the Google Play Store by generating a signed APK or Android App Bundle.

- Create a developer account on the Google Play Console, complete the necessary app store listing details, and upload your app's APK or App Bundle.

- Follow the submission and review process outlined by Google Play, ensuring compliance with store policies and guidelines.

By following these continued steps and best practices, you'll be able to develop, test, and deploy high-quality Android apps that provide value to users and contribute to the Android ecosystem. Keep learning, experimenting, and refining your skills to excel in Android app development.

21. **Monitor and Analyze App Performance**:

   - After publishing your app, monitor its performance using analytics tools provided by the Google Play Console or third-party services. Analyze metrics such as user engagement, retention rates, crash reports, and user feedback to identify areas for improvement and optimize your app accordingly.

   - Utilize A/B testing and experimentation techniques to compare different versions of your app and make data-driven decisions to enhance user experience and achieve your app's goals.

22. **Engage with Your User Community**:

   - Foster a strong relationship with your app's user community by responding promptly to user feedback, addressing concerns, and acknowledging feature requests. Engage with users through social media channels, community forums, and app review platforms to build trust and loyalty.

   - Encourage users to provide ratings and reviews for your app on the Google Play Store, as positive reviews can improve your app's visibility and credibility.

23. **Keep Your App Updated**:

- Regularly update your app with new features, bug fixes, performance improvements, and security patches to ensure a positive user experience and maintain competitiveness in the marketplace.

- Pay attention to user feedback, industry trends, and platform updates to identify opportunities for innovation and refinement in your app.

24. **Protect User Privacy and Data Security**:

- Prioritize user privacy and data security by implementing best practices for data handling, storage, and transmission in your app. Adhere to relevant privacy regulations such as the General Data Protection Regulation (GDPR) and ensure compliance with Google Play policies.

- Secure sensitive user data using encryption techniques, implement authentication mechanisms to protect user accounts, and regularly audit your app's security posture to mitigate risks.

25. **Continuously Learn and Improve**:

- Stay curious, proactive, and open-minded in your approach to Android app development. Continuously seek opportunities to learn new technologies, explore innovative solutions, and expand your skill set.

- Participate in professional development activities such as online courses, workshops, and certifications to deepen your expertise and stay abreast of industry advancements.

- Collaborate with peers, share knowledge, and contribute to the Android developer community to foster growth and collective learning.

By following these ongoing practices and principles, you'll be able to build successful, sustainable Android apps that resonate with users, drive engagement, and make a positive impact in the digital landscape. Keep iterating, adapting, and striving for excellence in your journey as an Android developer.

4

Design User Interface

Designing the user interface (UI) for your Android app involves creating visually appealing layouts that are intuitive to use and align with your app's functionality and branding. Here's an explanation of key UI design principles with examples:

1. **Consistency**:

   - Maintain consistency in the design elements, such as colors, typography, icons, and layout, throughout your app to provide a cohesive user experience.

   - Example: Use consistent color schemes and typography across different screens and components in your app.

2. **Simplicity**:

   - Keep the UI simple and uncluttered to avoid overwhelming users with unnecessary elements or information.

- Example: Use clean and minimalistic designs with ample white space to reduce visual clutter.

3. **Navigation**:
   - Design intuitive navigation patterns that allow users to easily move between different sections of your app and access key features.
   - Example: Use a bottom navigation bar, tabs, or a drawer menu to provide clear navigation options.

4. **Visual Hierarchy**:
   - Organize UI elements in a hierarchy based on their importance, emphasizing primary actions and content while de-emphasizing secondary or less critical elements.
   - Example: Use larger font sizes, bold text, or prominent buttons to highlight primary actions such as "Sign Up" or "Purchase."

5. **Feedback**:
   - Provide visual feedback to users when they interact with UI elements, such as buttons, links, or form fields, to indicate that their actions have been acknowledged.
   - Example: Change the color or appearance of a button when it's pressed to indicate that it has been tapped.

6. **Accessibility**:

   - Design your app to be accessible to users with disabilities by ensuring that UI elements are perceivable, operable, and understandable.

   - Example: Use descriptive labels for images and buttons to assist users who rely on screen readers.

7. **Responsive Design**:

   - Create layouts that adapt to different screen sizes and orientations, ensuring a consistent user experience across a variety of devices.

   - Example: Use ConstraintLayout or RelativeLayout to create flexible layouts that adjust dynamically based on screen size and resolution.

8. **Typography**:

   - Choose appropriate fonts, font sizes, and text styles to enhance readability and convey information effectively.

   - Example: Use a sans-serif font for body text and a bold serif font for headings to create contrast and hierarchy.

9. **Color Scheme**:

   - Select a cohesive color scheme that reflects your app's brand identity and creates a visually appealing atmosphere.

   - Example: Use complementary or analogous colors to create harmony and balance in your app's design.

10. **User Testing**:

- Conduct usability testing with real users to gather feedback on your app's UI design, identify pain points, and iteratively improve the user experience.

- Example: Conduct user interviews, surveys, or usability studies to gather qualitative and quantitative feedback on your app's UI.

By applying these UI design principles and examples, you can create user-friendly and visually engaging interfaces that enhance the usability and appeal of your Android app. Remember to iterate on your designs based on user feedback and testing results to continuously improve the user experience.

11. **Content Layout**:

- Organize content in a logical and intuitive manner to guide users through your app's interface and facilitate their interaction with information.

- Example: Group related content together, use meaningful headings and section titles, and prioritize important information for easy comprehension.

12. **Interactive Elements**:

- Design interactive elements such as buttons, icons, and gestures to be easily recognizable and responsive to user input.

- Example: Use standard Android UI components like FloatingActionButton for primary actions, and ensure that buttons change appearance when tapped to provide visual feedback.

13. **Error Handling**:

- Design error messages and alerts that clearly communicate issues to users and provide guidance on how to resolve them.

- Example: Display a toast message or a Snackbar with a descriptive error message when a user enters invalid input in a form field.

14. **Adaptability to Different Screen Sizes and Orientations**:

- Ensure that your app's UI layout and components adapt gracefully to various screen sizes, resolutions, and orientations to provide a consistent experience across devices.

- Example: Use ConstraintLayout to create responsive layouts that automatically adjust based on screen size and orientation, and provide alternative layouts for landscape and portrait modes if necessary.

15. **Brand Identity**:

- Reflect your app's brand identity through visual elements such as colors, logos, and imagery to create a cohesive and memorable user experience.

- Example: Use your app's logo and brand colors consistently throughout the UI, and incorporate branding elements into UI components like buttons and icons.

16. **User Feedback Mechanisms**:

- Incorporate mechanisms for users to provide feedback, suggestions, and ratings directly within the app to foster engagement and improve user satisfaction.

- Example: Include a "Send Feedback" option in the app's settings menu, or prompt users to rate the app after completing a significant action or task.

17. **Progress Indicators**:

- Use progress indicators, such as spinners, progress bars, animations, to provide feedback to users when tasks are in progress or loading.

- Example: Display a progress bar when downloading or uploading files, and use a spinner to indicate that content is being loaded dynamically.

18. **Accessibility Features**:

   - Implement accessibility features such as screen reader support, text-to-speech capabilities, and alternative input methods to ensure that your app is usable by all users, including those with disabilities.

   - Example: Provide descriptive alt text for images, enable high-contrast mode, and ensure that UI elements can be navigated and interacted with using keyboard shortcuts or gestures.

By incorporating these additional UI design considerations and examples into your app development process, you can create interfaces that are not only visually appealing but also intuitive, accessible, and user-friendly for a diverse audience of Android users.

19. **Gesture-Based Interactions**:

   - Integrate gesture-based interactions to enhance user engagement and streamline navigation within your app. Common gestures include swiping, tapping, pinching, and dragging.

   - Example: Implement swipe gestures to navigate between tabs or screens, or use pinch-to-zoom gestures to interact with images or maps.

20. **Personalization and Customization**:

- Provide users with options to personalize their app experience by customizing settings, themes, or layouts according to their preferences.

- Example: Allow users to choose between light and dark themes, customize the app's color scheme, or rearrange UI elements to suit their workflow.

21. **Microinteractions**:

- Incorporate subtle animations, transitions, and feedback mechanisms known as microinteractions to add polish and delight to your app's UI.

- Example: Use animated icons for loading indicators, implement smooth transitions between screens, or add subtle visual effects when elements are interacted with.

22. **Offline Support**:

- Design your app's UI to gracefully handle offline scenarios by providing users with informative messages, caching data, or offering limited offline functionality.

- Example: Display a message indicating that the app is offline and prompt users to try again later when attempting to access online content without an internet connection.

23. **Multi-Language Support**:

- Enable multi-language support in your app's UI to cater to users from diverse linguistic backgrounds. Provide translations for UI text and content to ensure accessibility and inclusivity.

- Example: Localize UI elements, such as buttons, labels, and error messages, into different languages based on the user's device language preferences.

24. **Dynamic Theming and Dark Mode**:

- Implement dynamic theming and support for dark mode to offer users flexibility in choosing their preferred visual appearance for the app. Dark mode can enhance readability and reduce eye strain in low-light environments.

- Example: Allow users to switch between light and dark modes in the app's settings, and automatically adapt the UI's color scheme based on system preferences.

25. **User Onboarding and Tutorials**:

- Design intuitive onboarding experiences and tutorials to help new users familiarize themselves with your app's features, functionality, and navigation. Keep the onboarding process concise and engaging to encourage user retention.

- Example: Use walkthroughs, tooltips, or interactive tutorials to guide users through key actions and interactions within the app during their first-time use.

By integrating these advanced UI design considerations and examples into your app development process, you can create engaging, user-centric interfaces that deliver a seamless and delightful user experience on the Android platform.

26. **Dynamic Content Loading**:

- Design your app's UI to efficiently load and display dynamic content from remote servers or databases. Utilize placeholders, lazy loading, and pagination techniques to optimize performance and provide a smooth user experience, especially when dealing with large datasets.

- Example: Implement a RecyclerView with a loading spinner or placeholder images while fetching and displaying content from an online feed. Use pagination to fetch additional content as the user scrolls through the list.

27. **In-App Notifications**:

- Incorporate in-app notifications to keep users informed about important events, updates, or actions within the app. Use banners, toasts, or modal dialogs to convey notifications effectively without disrupting the user's workflow.

- Example: Display a toast message confirming a successful action (e.g., "Item added to cart") or show a banner notification for new messages or alerts within the app.

28. **App Bar and Toolbar**:

- Design a consistent app bar and toolbar layout that provides easy access to navigation, search, and other essential actions. Use app bar components like the toolbar, action bar, and menu options to organize functionality and maintain navigation hierarchy.

- Example: Place navigation icons, search functionality, and action buttons (e.g., "Add", "Edit") within the app bar to facilitate common user interactions and tasks.

29. **Responsive Typography**:

- Optimize typography for readability and legibility across different screen sizes and resolutions. Choose font sizes, line spacing, and text styles that adapt dynamically to accommodate varying screen dimensions and user preferences.

- Example: Use scalable font sizes and responsive typography techniques to ensure that text remains clear and readable on devices with different screen sizes, densities, and aspect ratios.

30. **App Theming and Branding**:

- Customize your app's visual appearance and branding to create a unique and memorable identity. Define a cohesive color palette, typography styles, and iconography that reflect your brand's personality and resonate with your target audience.

 - Example: Incorporate brand colors, logos, and visual elements into the app's UI design, including splash screens, icons, and themed components, to reinforce brand recognition and create a cohesive brand experience.

By incorporating these advanced UI design concepts and examples into your Android app development process, you can create immersive, intuitive, and visually stunning user interfaces that captivate users and elevate the overall user experience. Remember to prioritize user feedback, iterate on your designs, and stay updated with emerging design trends to continuously refine and enhance your app's UI.

5

Write Code

Certainly! Let's cover some basic Android app development code examples using Java in Android Studio:

1. **Creating a Button with Click Event**:

```java
// MainActivity.java

import android.os.Bundle;
import android.view.View;
import android.widget.Button;
import android.widget.Toast;
import androidx.appcompat.app.AppCompatActivity;

public class MainActivity extends AppCompatActivity {
```

```java
    @Override
    protected void onCreate(Bundle savedInstanceState) {
    super.onCreate(savedInstanceState);
    setContentView(R.layout.activity_main);

Button button = findViewById(R.id.button);
    button.setOnClickListener(new   View.OnClickListener()
{
    @Override
    public void onClick(View v) {
    // Display a toast message when the button is clicked
    Toast.makeText(MainActivity.this,   "Button   Clicked",
Toast.LENGTH_SHORT).show();
    }
    });
    }
    }
    ```
```

```xml
    <!— activity_main.xml —>

<?xml version="1.0" encoding="utf-8"?>
    <RelativeLayout
xmlns:android="http://schemas.android.com/apk/res/android
"
```
```

```
    xmlns:tools="http://schemas.android.com/tools"
    android:layout_width="match_parent"
    android:layout_height="match_parent"
    android:padding="16dp"
    tools:context=".MainActivity">

<Button
    android:id="@+id/button"
    android:layout_width="wrap_content"
    android:layout_height="wrap_content"
    android:text="Click Me" />

</RelativeLayout>
```

2. **Displaying Text in TextView**:

```java
// MainActivity.java

import android.os.Bundle;
import android.widget.TextView;
import androidx.appcompat.app.AppCompatActivity;

public class MainActivity extends AppCompatActivity {
```

```
@Override
    protected void onCreate(Bundle savedInstanceState) {
    super.onCreate(savedInstanceState);
    setContentView(R.layout.activity_main);

TextView textView = findViewById(R.id.textView);
    textView.setText("Hello, World!");
    }
    }
    ```
```

```xml
    <!— activity_main.xml —>

<?xml version="1.0" encoding="utf-8"?>
    <RelativeLayout
xmlns:android="http://schemas.android.com/apk/res/android
"

    xmlns:tools="http://schemas.android.com/tools"
    android:layout_width="match_parent"
    android:layout_height="match_parent"
    android:padding="16dp"
    tools:context=".MainActivity">

 <TextView
    android:id="@+id/textView"
```
```

```
    android:layout_width="wrap_content"
    android:layout_height="wrap_content"
    android:text="TextView" />

</RelativeLayout>
```

These examples demonstrate basic UI components (Button, TextView) and event handling in Android using Java. You can copy and paste these code snippets into your Android project in Android Studio to see them in action. Remember to replace `MainActivity` and `activity_main` with your actual class and layout names.

3. **Handling EditText Input and Displaying in TextView**:

```java
// MainActivity.java

import android.os.Bundle;
import android.text.Editable;
import android.text.TextWatcher;
import android.widget.EditText;
import android.widget.TextView;
import androidx.appcompat.app.AppCompatActivity;
```

```java
public class MainActivity extends AppCompatActivity {

private EditText editText;
    private TextView textView;

@Override
    protected void onCreate(Bundle savedInstanceState) {
        super.onCreate(savedInstanceState);
        setContentView(R.layout.activity_main);

editText = findViewById(R.id.editText);
        textView = findViewById(R.id.textView);

editText.addTextChangedListener(new TextWatcher() {
        @Override
        public void beforeTextChanged(CharSequence s, int start, int count, int after) {}

@Override
        public void onTextChanged(CharSequence s, int start, int before, int count) {
        // Update the TextView with the text entered in the EditText
        textView.setText(s);
        }
```

```
@Override
    public void afterTextChanged(Editable s) {}
    });
    }
    }
    ```
```

```xml
    <!— activity_main.xml —>

<?xml version="1.0" encoding="utf-8"?>
    <RelativeLayout
xmlns:android="http://schemas.android.com/apk/res/android"

    xmlns:tools="http://schemas.android.com/tools"
    android:layout_width="match_parent"
    android:layout_height="match_parent"
    android:padding="16dp"
    tools:context=".MainActivity">

<EditText
    android:id="@+id/editText"
    android:layout_width="match_parent"
    android:layout_height="wrap_content"
    android:hint="Enter text"/>
```
```

```xml
<TextView
    android:id="@+id/textView"
    android:layout_width="wrap_content"
    android:layout_height="wrap_content"
    android:layout_below="@id/editText"
    android:layout_marginTop="16dp"
    android:text="TextView"/>

</RelativeLayout>
```


4. **Launching a New Activity on Button Click**:

```java
// MainActivity.java

import android.content.Intent;
import android.os.Bundle;
import android.view.View;
import android.widget.Button;
import androidx.appcompat.app.AppCompatActivity;

public class MainActivity extends AppCompatActivity {
```

```java
    @Override
    protected void onCreate(Bundle savedInstanceState) {
        super.onCreate(savedInstanceState);
        setContentView(R.layout.activity_main);

Button button = findViewById(R.id.button);
        button.setOnClickListener(new   View.OnClickListener()
{
        @Override
        public void onClick(View v) {
        // Launch a new activity when the button is clicked
        Intent    intent    =    new    Intent(MainActivity.this,
SecondActivity.class);
        startActivity(intent);
        }
        });
        }
        }
```


```java
    // SecondActivity.java

import android.os.Bundle;
    import androidx.appcompat.app.AppCompatActivity;
```

```java
public class SecondActivity extends AppCompatActivity {

@Override
    protected void onCreate(Bundle savedInstanceState) {
    super.onCreate(savedInstanceState);
    setContentView(R.layout.activity_second);
    }
    }
    ```


```xml
    <!— activity_main.xml —>

<!— Assume you have a Button with id "button" —>

<!— activity_second.xml —>

<!— Layout for the second activity —>
    ```
```
```

These examples illustrate more advanced interactions and functionalities in Android app development, including handling EditText input, updating TextView dynamically, and launching a new activity. You can incorporate these code snippets into your Android project to implement similar features in your app.

5. **Using RecyclerView to Display a List of Items**:

```java
    // MainActivity.java

import android.os.Bundle;
    import androidx.appcompat.app.AppCompatActivity;
    import
androidx.recyclerview.widget.LinearLayoutManager;
    import androidx.recyclerview.widget.RecyclerView;

import java.util.ArrayList;
    import java.util.List;

public class MainActivity extends AppCompatActivity {

private RecyclerView recyclerView;
    private RecyclerViewAdapter adapter;
```

```java
    private List<String> itemList;

@Override
    protected void onCreate(Bundle savedInstanceState) {
    super.onCreate(savedInstanceState);
    setContentView(R.layout.activity_main);

recyclerView = findViewById(R.id.recyclerView);
    itemList = new ArrayList<>();
    // Populate itemList with dummy data
    itemList.add("Item 1");
    itemList.add("Item 2");
    itemList.add("Item 3");
    // Initialize RecyclerView and set adapter
    adapter = new RecyclerViewAdapter(itemList);
    recyclerView.setLayoutManager(new
LinearLayoutManager(this));
    recyclerView.setAdapter(adapter);
    }
    }
```

```java
    // RecyclerViewAdapter.java
```

```java
import android.view.LayoutInflater;
import android.view.View;
import android.view.ViewGroup;
import android.widget.TextView;
import androidx.annotation.NonNull;
import androidx.recyclerview.widget.RecyclerView;
import java.util.List;

public class RecyclerViewAdapter extends
RecyclerView.Adapter<RecyclerViewAdapter.ViewHolder>
{

private List<String> itemList;

public RecyclerViewAdapter(List<String> itemList) {
    this.itemList = itemList;
    }


@NonNull
    @Override
    public ViewHolder onCreateViewHolder(@NonNull
ViewGroup parent, int viewType) {
    View view =
LayoutInflater.from(parent.getContext()).inflate(R.layout.ite
m_layout, parent, false);
    return new ViewHolder(view);
```

```java
    }

@Override
    public void onBindViewHolder(@NonNull ViewHolder
holder, int position) {
        String item = itemList.get(position);
        holder.textView.setText(item);
    }

@Override
    public int getItemCount() {
        return itemList.size();
    }

public class ViewHolder extends RecyclerView.ViewHolder
{
        TextView textView;

public ViewHolder(@NonNull View itemView) {
        super(itemView);
        textView = itemView.findViewById(R.id.textView);
    }
    }
    }
    ```
```
```

```xml
<!-- item_layout.xml -->

<TextView
xmlns:android="http://schemas.android.com/apk/res/android"

    android:id="@+id/textView"
    android:layout_width="match_parent"
    android:layout_height="wrap_content"
    android:padding="16dp"
    android:textSize="16sp"/>
```

```xml
<!-- activity_main.xml -->

<?xml version="1.0" encoding="utf-8"?>
    <RelativeLayout
xmlns:android="http://schemas.android.com/apk/res/android"

    xmlns:tools="http://schemas.android.com/tools"
    android:layout_width="match_parent"
    android:layout_height="match_parent"
    android:padding="16dp"
    tools:context=".MainActivity">
```

```
<androidx.recyclerview.widget.RecyclerView
    android:id="@+id/recyclerView"
    android:layout_width="match_parent"
    android:layout_height="match_parent"/>

</RelativeLayout>
```

This example demonstrates how to use RecyclerView to display a list of items in an Android app. The RecyclerViewAdapter class handles the creation and binding of views for each item in the list, while the item layout (item_layout.xml) defines the appearance of individual list items. You can customize the RecyclerViewAdapter to display any type of data and implement additional features such as item click listeners.

6. **Handling Item Clicks in RecyclerView**:

```java
// RecyclerViewAdapter.java

import android.view.LayoutInflater;
import android.view.View;
import android.view.ViewGroup;
```

```java
import android.widget.TextView;
import androidx.annotation.NonNull;
import androidx.recyclerview.widget.RecyclerView;
import java.util.List;

public class RecyclerViewAdapter extends
RecyclerView.Adapter<RecyclerViewAdapter.ViewHolder>
{

private List<String> itemList;
    private OnItemClickListener listener;

public interface OnItemClickListener {
    void onItemClick(String item);
    }

public RecyclerViewAdapter(List<String> itemList,
OnItemClickListener listener) {
    this.itemList = itemList;
    this.listener = listener;
    }

@NonNull
    @Override
    public ViewHolder onCreateViewHolder(@NonNull
ViewGroup parent, int viewType) {
```

```java
    View                    view                    =
LayoutInflater.from(parent.getContext()).inflate(R.layout.ite
m_layout, parent, false);
    return new ViewHolder(view);
    }


@Override
    public void onBindViewHolder(@NonNull ViewHolder
holder, int position) {
    String item = itemList.get(position);
    holder.textView.setText(item);
    holder.bind(item, listener);
    }


@Override
    public int getItemCount() {
    return itemList.size();
    }


public class ViewHolder extends RecyclerView.ViewHolder
{
    TextView textView;


public ViewHolder(@NonNull View itemView) {
    super(itemView);
    textView = itemView.findViewById(R.id.textView);
```

```java
    }

    public void bind(final String item, final OnItemClickListener listener) {
        itemView.setOnClickListener(new View.OnClickListener() {
            @Override
            public void onClick(View v) {
                // Pass the clicked item to the onItemClick method of the listener
                listener.onItemClick(item);
            }
        });
    }
}
```

```java
// MainActivity.java

import android.os.Bundle;
import androidx.appcompat.app.AppCompatActivity;
import androidx.recyclerview.widget.LinearLayoutManager;
import androidx.recyclerview.widget.RecyclerView;
```

```java
import java.util.ArrayList;
import java.util.List;

public class MainActivity extends AppCompatActivity {

private RecyclerView recyclerView;
    private RecyclerViewAdapter adapter;
    private List<String> itemList;

@Override
    protected void onCreate(Bundle savedInstanceState) {
    super.onCreate(savedInstanceState);
    setContentView(R.layout.activity_main);

recyclerView = findViewById(R.id.recyclerView);
    itemList = new ArrayList<>();
    itemList.add("Item 1");
    itemList.add("Item 2");
    itemList.add("Item 3");

adapter    =    new    RecyclerViewAdapter(itemList,    new
RecyclerViewAdapter.OnItemClickListener() {
    @Override
    public void onItemClick(String item) {
    // Handle item click event
    }
```

```
    });

recyclerView.setLayoutManager(new
LinearLayoutManager(this));
    recyclerView.setAdapter(adapter);
    }
    }
    ```
```

In this example, we've added functionality to handle item clicks in the RecyclerView. The RecyclerViewAdapter now includes an interface `OnItemClickListener` and a method `bind()` in the ViewHolder class to handle item click events. In the MainActivity, we pass an instance of `OnItemClickListener` to the RecyclerViewAdapter constructor, allowing us to implement the `onItemClick()` method to respond to item clicks. You can customize the onItemClick() method to perform any action when an item in the RecyclerView is clicked, such as navigating to a new activity or updating UI elements.
```

6

Test Your App

Testing your Android app is crucial to ensure its functionality, usability, and performance. Here are various types of testing and how to perform them:

1. **Unit Testing**:
   - Unit tests verify the functionality of individual units or components of your app in isolation.
   - Example: Testing a method that performs a calculation or a function that validates user input.
   - Use JUnit and AndroidX Test libraries to write and execute unit tests within Android Studio.

2. **Integration Testing**:
   - Integration tests verify interactions between different components or modules within your app.
   - Example: Testing the interaction between UI components and database operations.

- Use frameworks like Espresso for UI testing and Mockito for mocking dependencies to facilitate integration testing.

3. **UI Testing**:
   - UI tests validate the behavior and appearance of your app's user interface across different devices and screen sizes.
   - Example: Testing navigation flows, button clicks, and text input in various UI screens.
   - Write UI tests using Espresso or UI Automator framework and run them using the AndroidJUnitRunner.

4. **End-to-End (E2E) Testing**:
   - E2E tests simulate real-world user scenarios to validate the entire app flow from start to finish.
   - Example: Testing the registration process, login functionality, and performing actions across multiple screens.
   - Use frameworks like Appium or Firebase Test Lab to automate E2E tests on physical devices or emulators.

5. **Performance Testing**:
   - Performance tests evaluate the responsiveness, resource usage, and stability of your app under different conditions.
   - Example: Testing app startup time, memory usage, and network latency.

- Use Android Profiler or third-party performance monitoring tools to analyze your app's performance metrics and identify bottlenecks.

6. **User Acceptance Testing (UAT)**:
    - UAT involves testing your app with real users to gather feedback, identify usability issues, and ensure that it meets their expectations.
    - Example: Conducting beta testing or alpha testing with a group of selected users before releasing the app to the public.
    - Distribute your app to testers using platforms like Google Play Console's internal testing track or third-party beta testing services.

7. **Accessibility Testing**:
    - Accessibility tests ensure that your app is usable by people with disabilities and adheres to accessibility guidelines and standards.
    - Example: Testing screen reader compatibility, keyboard navigation, and contrast ratio for visually impaired users.
    - Use accessibility testing tools provided by Android Studio or third-party accessibility testing services to evaluate your app's accessibility features.

8. **Security Testing**:

   - Security tests assess your app's vulnerability to common security threats, such as data breaches, unauthorized access, and malicious attacks.

   - Example: Testing input validation, encryption methods, and secure communication protocols.

   - Use static code analysis tools, penetration testing, and security scanning services to identify and address security vulnerabilities in your app.

By implementing a comprehensive testing strategy that includes various types of tests, you can ensure the reliability, performance, and user satisfaction of your Android app. Continuously iterate on your testing process based on feedback and evolving requirements to deliver a high-quality app to your users.

9. **Localization Testing**:

   - Localization tests verify that your app's user interface and content are accurately translated and culturally appropriate for different languages and regions.

   - Example: Testing text alignment, date formats, and currency symbols in localized versions of your app.

- Use localization testing tools or manually review localized versions of your app to ensure linguistic and cultural accuracy.

10. **Device Compatibility Testing**:

- Device compatibility tests ensure that your app functions correctly on a wide range of Android devices with varying hardware specifications, screen sizes, and software configurations.

- Example: Testing your app on different devices from various manufacturers, including smartphones, tablets, and wearable devices.

- Use emulators, physical devices, and cloud-based testing services to verify device compatibility and identify any device-specific issues.

11. **Regression Testing**:

- Regression tests validate that recent code changes or updates to your app have not introduced new bugs or regressions in existing functionality.

- Example: Re-running previously executed test cases after making code modifications to verify that the app behaves as expected.

- Automate regression tests using testing frameworks and tools to quickly detect and address any unintended changes or defects.

12. **Robustness Testing**:

- Robustness tests assess your app's ability to handle unexpected inputs, errors, and adverse conditions gracefully without crashing or malfunctioning.

- Example: Simulating low memory conditions, network disruptions, or invalid user inputs to evaluate the app's resilience.

- Use stress testing, boundary testing, and fault injection techniques to subject your app to challenging scenarios and verify its robustness.

13. **Usability Testing**:

- Usability tests evaluate the overall user experience and ease of use of your app by observing how users interact with it and soliciting feedback on its design and functionality.

- Example: Conducting usability studies, interviews, or surveys with target users to assess navigation flows, layout clarity, and task completion efficiency.

- Analyze user feedback and behavior patterns to identify usability issues and iteratively improve the app's design and user interface.

14. **Scalability Testing**:

   - Scalability tests assess your app's ability to handle increasing user loads, data volumes, and concurrent sessions without performance degradation or system failures.

   - Example: Simulating a surge in user traffic or data processing to evaluate the app's scalability and resource utilization.

   - Use load testing tools and performance monitoring techniques to measure your app's scalability limits and optimize its scalability characteristics.

15. **Documentation and Release Notes Review**:

   - Review the app's documentation, release notes, and user guides to ensure they accurately reflect the app's features, functionality, and changes introduced in each release.

   - Example: Reviewing app documentation for completeness, accuracy, and clarity of instructions, troubleshooting steps, and version history.

   - Collaborate with technical writers, product managers, and QA team members to verify the accuracy and consistency of documentation materials before releasing the app to users.

By incorporating these additional testing practices into your app development lifecycle, you can enhance the quality, reliability, and usability of your Android app, ultimately delivering a positive user experience and maximizing user satisfaction.

16. **Automated Testing**:

- Implement automated testing frameworks and tools to streamline the testing process, increase test coverage, and accelerate feedback loops during development.

- Example: Use continuous integration (CI) platforms like Jenkins or CircleCI to automate the execution of unit tests, integration tests, and UI tests on every code commit.

- Integrate testing frameworks such as Espresso, Robolectric, and Mockito into your CI/CD pipeline to automate the execution of various test suites and generate test reports.

17. **Continuous Monitoring and Feedback**:

- Establish mechanisms for continuous monitoring of your app's performance, stability, and user feedback post-release to identify issues promptly and prioritize improvements.

- Example: Monitor app crashes, ANR (Application Not Responding) errors, and performance metrics using crash reporting tools like Firebase Crashlytics or Bugsnag.

- Collect and analyze user feedback, ratings, and reviews from app stores, social media platforms, and in-app feedback channels to gain insights into user satisfaction and areas for enhancement.

18. **Cross-Platform Compatibility Testing**:

- Verify that your app functions correctly on different versions of the Android operating system (OS) and is compatible with the latest platform features and APIs.

- Example: Test your app on various Android OS versions, including older versions (e.g., Android 4.x) and the latest releases (e.g., Android 12), to ensure backward and forward compatibility.

- Leverage Android emulator snapshots and virtual devices to simulate different OS configurations and screen densities for comprehensive compatibility testing.

19. **Code Review and Quality Assurance**:

- Conduct code reviews and quality assurance (QA) checks to ensure that your app's codebase adheres to coding standards, best practices, and architectural principles.

- Example: Perform peer code reviews using code review tools like GitHub Pull Requests or Bitbucket Code Insights to identify code smells, bugs, and performance bottlenecks early in the development cycle.

- Use static code analysis tools, code linters, and automated code review bots to enforce coding conventions, detect code vulnerabilities, and maintain code quality consistency across the project.

20. **User Behavior Analytics**:

- Leverage user behavior analytics and app usage metrics to gain insights into how users interact with your app, identify usage patterns, and make data-driven decisions to optimize user engagement and retention.

- Example: Integrate analytics SDKs such as Google Analytics or Firebase Analytics into your app to track user actions, session durations, conversion rates, and other key performance indicators (KPIs).

- Analyze user behavior data to identify user journey bottlenecks, optimize app flows, and personalize user experiences through targeted messaging, notifications, and content recommendations.

By integrating these advanced testing practices and feedback mechanisms into your Android app development workflow, you can establish a robust quality assurance process, improve app quality continuously, and deliver exceptional experiences to your users.

7

Optimize And Refine

Optimizing and refining your Android app involves fine-tuning its performance, usability, and user experience to ensure that it meets or exceeds user expectations. Here are some strategies and examples to achieve optimization and refinement:

1. **Performance Optimization**:

   - Identify and address performance bottlenecks, such as slow loading times, high memory usage, and excessive battery consumption, to enhance the overall responsiveness and efficiency of your app.

   - Example: Implementing lazy loading for images and data to improve initial app startup time and reduce memory overhead.

2. **UI/UX Refinement**:

   - Continuously iterate on your app's user interface and user experience to make it more intuitive, visually appealing, and engaging for users.

   - Example: Refining navigation flows, layout designs, and animation transitions based on user feedback and usability testing results.

3. **Codebase Optimization**:

   - Streamline and optimize your app's codebase by refactoring redundant or inefficient code, removing deprecated APIs, and adopting coding best practices to enhance maintainability and scalability.

   - Example: Consolidating duplicate code into reusable components or libraries to reduce code duplication and improve code modularity.

4. **Network and Data Optimization**:

   - Optimize network requests, data caching, and synchronization mechanisms to minimize data usage, reduce latency, and improve offline capabilities in your app.

   - Example: Implementing intelligent data caching strategies, such as caching frequently accessed data locally and prefetching resources in advance, to reduce network traffic and improve data loading times.

5. **Battery and Resource Efficiency**:

   - Optimize your app's power consumption and resource utilization to prolong device battery life and minimize resource contention with other apps running on the device.

   - Example: Implementing background task scheduling and job batching to reduce CPU wake-ups and optimize resource usage, especially for long-running background processes.

6. **Accessibility and Inclusivity Enhancements**:

   - Enhance the accessibility features and inclusivity of your app to ensure that it is usable by users with disabilities and diverse needs.

   - Example: Implementing screen reader support, keyboard navigation, and high-contrast themes to improve accessibility for users with visual impairments or motor disabilities.

7. **Localization and Internationalization**:

   - Localize and internationalize your app to support multiple languages, cultures, and regions, enabling users worldwide to access and use your app in their preferred language and locale.

   - Example: Providing translated app content, culturally relevant imagery, and localized date/time formats to accommodate users from different regions and language backgrounds.

8. **Security and Privacy Enhancements**:

   - Strengthen the security and privacy protections of your app by implementing robust authentication mechanisms, data encryption, and compliance with privacy regulations.

   - Example: Enforcing secure communication protocols (e.g., HTTPS) for network requests, implementing user consent mechanisms for data collection, and regularly auditing your app for security vulnerabilities.

By adopting these optimization and refinement strategies, you can elevate the quality, performance, and user satisfaction of your Android app, leading to increased user engagement, retention, and positive reviews in the Google Play Store. Continuously monitor user feedback and app analytics to identify areas for improvement and iterate on your app's design and functionality iteratively.

9. **Error Handling and Stability Improvements**:

   - Implement robust error handling mechanisms to gracefully handle unexpected errors, crashes, and exceptions, preventing app crashes and ensuring a stable user experience.

- Example: Implementing try-catch blocks, exception logging, and crash reporting tools to capture and report errors to developers for analysis and resolution.

10. **Optimized Images and Media Assets**:
   - Optimize images and media assets used in your app to reduce file size, improve loading times, and minimize bandwidth usage without sacrificing visual quality.
   - Example: Compressing images using tools like TinyPNG or WebP format conversion to achieve smaller file sizes while maintaining image quality.

11. **Memory Management and Garbage Collection**:
   - Optimize memory usage and garbage collection in your app to prevent memory leaks, reduce memory footprint, and improve overall performance and responsiveness.
   - Example: Using memory profiling tools like Android Profiler to identify memory leaks and optimizing resource-intensive operations to minimize memory usage.

12. **Feedback Mechanisms and User Engagement**:
   - Implement feedback mechanisms and interactive features in your app to solicit user feedback, encourage user engagement, and foster a sense of community among your users.

- Example: Integrating in-app feedback forms, surveys, and ratings prompts to gather user feedback and ratings, and responding promptly to user inquiries and suggestions.

13. **A/B Testing and Experimentation**:

- Conduct A/B testing and experimentation to evaluate different design variations, feature implementations, and user flows, enabling data-driven decision-making and optimization.

- Example: Using A/B testing frameworks like Firebase Remote Config or Google Optimize to experiment with different app layouts, content placements, and feature toggles to determine the most effective configurations.

14. **App Size Reduction**:

- Optimize your app's size and reduce its footprint on users' devices by removing unused resources, optimizing code and libraries, and leveraging app bundle delivery for dynamic delivery of resources.

- Example: Analyzing APK size using tools like Android Studio's APK Analyzer and ProGuard for code obfuscation and minification to reduce the size of the app package.

15. **Performance Profiling and Benchmarking**:

- Conduct performance profiling and benchmarking of your app to identify performance bottlenecks, measure your app to identify performance bottlenecks, measure improvements, and set performance targets for optimization efforts.

- Example: Using performance monitoring tools like Android Studio Profiler or third-party benchmarking tools to measure app startup time, rendering performance, and CPU usage under various conditions.

By implementing these optimization and refinement strategies, you can continuously improve your Android app's performance, stability, usability, and user satisfaction, resulting in a more polished and compelling user experience. Regularly monitor app performance metrics, user feedback, and analytics data to identify areas for further optimization and refinement iteratively.

16. **User-Centric Updates and Iterations**:
    - Prioritize user feedback and feature requests to guide the direction of app updates and iterations, focusing on addressing user needs and pain points to enhance user satisfaction.
    - Example: Analyzing user feedback from app reviews, support channels, and user surveys to identify common issues or feature requests and incorporating them into the app roadmap for future updates.

17. **Continuous Learning and Skill Development**:

- Invest in continuous learning and skill development to stay updated with the latest trends, technologies, and best practices in Android app development, enabling you to adopt new tools and techniques for optimization and refinement.

- Example: Participating in online courses, attending conferences, and joining developer communities to expand your knowledge and expertise in areas such as performance optimization, UI/UX design, and emerging technologies.

18. **Competitive Analysis and Benchmarking**:

- Conduct competitive analysis and benchmarking to compare your app's performance, features, and user experience against competitors' apps, identifying areas for differentiation and improvement.

- Example: Evaluating competitors' apps in the same category, analyzing their strengths and weaknesses, and leveraging market insights to enhance your app's competitive edge and value proposition.

19. **Data-Driven Decision Making**:

- Base optimization and refinement decisions on data-driven insights, leveraging analytics data, user behavior metrics, and performance indicators to prioritize initiatives and measure their impact on app performance and user satisfaction.

- Example: Using A/B testing, cohort analysis, and user segmentation to assess the effectiveness of app optimizations, feature enhancements, and UI/UX changes and make informed decisions based on empirical evidence.

20. **Community Engagement and Collaboration**:
   - Foster a sense of community engagement and collaboration among users, developers, and stakeholders, encouraging open communication, feedback sharing, and collaborative problem-solving to drive continuous improvement and innovation.
   - Example: Establishing developer forums, organizing user meetups, and participating in open-source projects to engage with the developer community, share knowledge and best practices, and collaborate on app improvement initiatives.

By embracing a holistic approach to optimization and refinement, encompassing user feedback, continuous learning, competitive analysis, data-driven decision-making, and community collaboration, you can create a vibrant and thriving ecosystem around your Android app, driving ongoing improvement and innovation to deliver exceptional value to your users.

21. **Regular Maintenance and Updates**:

- Commit to regular maintenance and updates for your Android app to address bug fixes, security vulnerabilities, and compatibility issues, ensuring that your app remains stable, secure, and compatible with evolving platform requirements.

- Example: Releasing periodic updates with bug fixes, security patches, and performance improvements based on user feedback, bug reports, and platform updates to maintain the app's reliability and relevance over time.

22. **User Education and Onboarding**:

- Provide comprehensive user education and onboarding materials to help users understand your app's features, functionality, and value proposition, facilitating seamless adoption and engagement.

- Example: Creating in-app tutorials, walkthroughs, and help documentation to guide users through key app features and workflows, addressing common user questions and concerns.

23. **Community Building and Engagement**:

- Foster a sense of community around your Android app by actively engaging with users, responding to their feedback and inquiries, and creating opportunities for user collaboration and participation.

- Example: Establishing user forums, social media groups, and developer communities to facilitate discussions, feature requests, and user-generated content related to your app, fostering a sense of belonging and loyalty among users.

24. **User Retention and Loyalty Programs**:
   - Implement user retention strategies and loyalty programs to incentivize continued engagement and usage of your app, rewarding loyal users and encouraging them to become advocates for your app.
   - Example: Offering rewards, discounts, or exclusive content to long-term users, implementing referral programs, and acknowledging user milestones to strengthen user retention and foster brand loyalty.

25. **Feedback Loops and Iterative Improvement**:
   - Establish feedback loops and iterative improvement processes to continuously gather user feedback, evaluate app performance, and prioritize enhancement opportunities, enabling ongoing refinement and optimization of your app.
   - Example: Collecting user feedback through in-app surveys, feedback forms, and usability testing sessions, analyzing feedback trends, and incorporating actionable insights into future app updates and iterations.

26. **Performance Monitoring and Optimization**:

- Implement robust performance monitoring and optimization practices to proactively identify and address performance issues, bottlenecks, and inefficiencies in your app, ensuring optimal performance and user experience.

- Example: Monitoring app performance metrics such as CPU usage, memory consumption, and network latency using performance monitoring tools and profiling techniques, optimizing code, and resource usage to improve app responsiveness and efficiency.

By incorporating these ongoing optimization and refinement strategies into your Android app lifecycle, you can cultivate a loyal user base, drive continuous improvement, and position your app for long-term success and sustainability in the competitive app market.

8

Publish Your App

Publishing your Android app involves preparing it for release, creating a Google Play Developer account, and uploading your app to the Google Play Store. Here's a step-by-step guide along with examples:

1. **Prepare Your App for Release**:
   - Ensure that your app is thoroughly tested, optimized, and meets all the necessary requirements for publication, including compliance with Google Play policies, proper functionality across different devices, and adherence to quality standards.

2. **Create a Google Play Developer Account**:
   - Sign up for a Google Play Developer account by visiting the Google Play Console website (https://play.google.com/console) and following the

instructions to create a new account or use an existing Google account.

- Complete the registration process by providing the required information, agreeing to the terms and conditions, and paying the one-time registration fee (if applicable).

3. **Generate a Signed APK or App Bundle**:

- Generate a signed APK (Android Package) or an Android App Bundle (.aab) file for your app using Android Studio's "Generate Signed Bundle / APK" option.

- Follow the wizard to configure your signing key, build type, and destination directory for the signed APK or bundle.

4. **Prepare Your App Listing**:

- Create a compelling app listing on the Google Play Console, including a catchy app title, informative description, high-quality screenshots, captivating promotional images or videos, and relevant app metadata (category, keywords, etc.).

- Provide detailed information about your app's features, functionality, and any necessary permissions required for installation and usage.

5. **Upload Your App to the Google Play Console**:

- Log in to your Google Play Console account and navigate to the "All apps" section.

- Click on the "Create app" button and follow the prompts to provide basic information about your app, such as its default language, title, and package name.

- Upload your signed APK or app bundle file, along with the necessary assets (screenshots, icons, promotional graphics) and metadata, to the app's listing page.

6. **Set Pricing and Distribution Options**:

- Choose whether to offer your app for free or set a price for it, and select the appropriate distribution options (global availability, country-specific availability, or closed alpha/beta testing) based on your app's target audience and release strategy.

- Configure monetization options such as in-app purchases, subscriptions, or ads if applicable to your app's business model.

7. **Review and Publish Your App**:

- Review the information provided on the app's listing page to ensure accuracy and completeness, and verify that your app complies with all Google Play policies and guidelines.

- Click on the "Submit" or "Publish" button to submit your app for review by the Google Play team.

- Once your app passes the review process and meets all the necessary requirements, it will be published on the

Google Play Store and made available to users for download and installation.

8. **Promote Your App**:

   - Promote your app through various channels, including social media, email newsletters, press releases, and app review websites, to increase visibility and attract users to download and try your app.

   - Encourage satisfied users to leave positive reviews and ratings on the Google Play Store to improve your app's reputation and discoverability among potential users.

By following these steps and best practices, you can successfully publish your Android app on the Google Play Store and reach a wide audience of potential users. Remember to keep your app updated with new features, bug fixes, and enhancements to maintain user engagement and satisfaction over time.

9. **Manage App Releases and Updates**:

   - Regularly update your app with new features, bug fixes, and performance improvements to keep it relevant, competitive, and up-to-date with user expectations and industry trends.

- Use the "Release management" section in the Google Play Console to manage app releases, create release channels (e.g., alpha, beta, production), and roll out updates to different user groups in a staged manner.

- Monitor user feedback, crash reports, and app performance metrics after each release to gather insights, identify issues, and prioritize improvements for future updates.

10. **Optimize App Store Optimization (ASO)**:

- Optimize your app store listing and metadata (e.g., title, description, keywords) to improve its visibility, ranking, and discoverability in the Google Play Store search results and category listings.

- Conduct keyword research, A/B test different listing elements, and monitor competitor strategies to continuously refine your ASO strategy and attract more organic traffic to your app's listing.

11. **Monitor and Analyze App Performance**:

- Use analytics tools provided by the Google Play Console or third-party analytics platforms to track key performance indicators (KPIs) such as downloads, active users, retention rates, and revenue.

- Analyze user engagement patterns, conversion funnels, and user demographics to gain insights into user behavior, preferences, and trends, and make data-driven decisions to optimize your app's performance and user experience.

12. **Engage with Your User Community**:

- Foster a strong relationship with your app's user community by actively engaging with users, responding to their feedback, addressing their concerns, and soliciting their input for future updates and features.

- Leverage in-app communication channels (e.g., feedback forms, support tickets, community forums) and social media platforms to interact with users, build trust, and cultivate a loyal user base around your app.

13. **Stay Compliant with Policies and Guidelines**:

- Stay informed about changes to Google Play policies, guidelines, and developer requirements, and ensure that your app remains compliant with all applicable regulations and standards.

- Regularly review and update your app's privacy policy, terms of service, and content guidelines to reflect any changes in your app's features, data collection practices, or legal requirements.

14. **Continuous Improvement and Innovation**:

- Embrace a culture of continuous improvement and innovation by seeking feedback from users, experimenting with new features and technologies, and iterating on your app's design and functionality to stay ahead of the competition.

- Stay abreast of emerging trends, user preferences, and technological advancements in the mobile app industry, and adapt your app strategy accordingly to capitalize on new opportunities and address evolving user needs.

By adopting these ongoing app management practices, you can maximize the success and longevity of your Android app on the Google Play Store, drive user engagement and retention, and position your app for sustained growth and profitability in the competitive app marketplace.

15. **Monitor and Respond to User Feedback**:
   - Regularly monitor user reviews, ratings, and comments on the Google Play Store, as well as feedback received through in-app channels, to understand user sentiments and address any issues or concerns promptly.
   - Respond to user feedback in a timely and professional manner, acknowledging their feedback, providing assistance or clarification as needed, and demonstrating a commitment to improving the app based on user input.

16. **Implement User Feedback into Updates**:

- Actively incorporate user feedback and feature requests into your app's development roadmap and update schedule, prioritizing enhancements that align with user needs and preferences.

- Engage with users to gather feedback on proposed features or changes, conduct user testing and validation, and iterate on design and functionality based on user input to ensure that updates meet user expectations.

17. **Promotional Activities and Marketing Campaigns**:

- Plan and execute promotional activities and marketing campaigns to raise awareness of your app, attract new users, and drive downloads and installations.

- Utilize various marketing channels and tactics, such as social media advertising, influencer partnerships, email newsletters, and app store optimization (ASO), to reach your target audience and promote your app effectively.

18. **Track and Measure Key Performance Metrics**:

- Define key performance metrics (KPIs) and establish benchmarks to track the success of your app and measure the effectiveness of your marketing efforts and user engagement strategies.

- Use analytics tools to monitor KPIs such as user acquisition, retention rates, engagement metrics, conversion rates, and revenue generation, and analyze trends and patterns to identify areas for improvement and optimization.

19. **Iterative Testing and Optimization**:

   - Continuously test and iterate on different aspects of your app, including features, user interface (UI) elements, messaging, and pricing strategies, to identify what resonates most with your target audience and optimize performance accordingly.

   - Conduct A/B tests, multivariate testing, and user segmentation experiments to evaluate the impact of changes and refine your app's design, functionality, and user experience based on empirical data and user feedback.

20. **Stay Informed and Adapt to Market Trends**:

   - Stay informed about industry trends, market dynamics, and competitor strategies by monitoring industry publications, attending conferences and events, and participating in developer communities and forums.

   - Adapt your app strategy and roadmap based on market insights and emerging opportunities, leveraging new technologies, platform features, and monetization models to stay competitive and meet evolving user demands.

By implementing these ongoing optimization and growth strategies, you can drive sustained success and maximize the impact of your Android app on the Google Play Store, achieving long-term growth and profitability in the competitive mobile app market.

9

Conclusion

In conclusion, successfully publishing and managing an Android app on the Google Play Store requires a multifaceted approach encompassing meticulous planning, diligent execution, and ongoing optimization. By following the steps outlined in this guide, from initial development and testing to app promotion and user engagement, developers can navigate the complexities of the app ecosystem and position their apps for success. Continuous iteration, user-centricity, and responsiveness to market dynamics are key to maintaining relevance and driving sustained growth in the competitive app landscape. With dedication, creativity, and a commitment to delivering value to users, developers can unlock the full potential of their Android apps and leave a lasting impact on the millions of users who rely on the Google Play Store for their digital needs.

As technology evolves and user expectations continue to rise, the journey of app development is a dynamic one, filled with challenges and opportunities alike. Embracing a mindset of continuous improvement and innovation is essential for developers seeking long-term success in the ever-changing app market. By staying informed about industry trends, listening to user feedback, and adapting to evolving technologies, developers can not only create captivating Android apps but also cultivate thriving communities of engaged users. As we look ahead, the future of Android app development holds boundless potential for those willing to push the boundaries of creativity and innovation. Let us embark on this journey together, fueled by passion, ingenuity, and a relentless pursuit of excellence.

In the vast and vibrant landscape of the Google Play Store, each app represents a unique opportunity to make a difference in users' lives, whether it's solving a problem, providing entertainment, or offering a new perspective. As developers, our mission extends beyond just creating software – it's about crafting experiences that resonate deeply with users, leaving a lasting impression and fostering meaningful connections.

With every line of code we write, every design decision we make, and every interaction we facilitate, we have the power to shape the digital world in profound ways. Let's embrace this responsibility with enthusiasm and dedication, striving not only to meet but exceed the expectations of our users at every turn.

As we embark on this journey of Android app development, let's remember that our greatest achievements are yet to come. Together, let's push the boundaries of what's possible, inspire one another, and leave a legacy that will endure for generations to come. The future of Android app development is bright, and the possibilities are limitless – let's seize them with passion, purpose, and unwavering determination.

www.ingramcontent.com/pod-product-compliance
Lightning Source LLC
Chambersburg PA
CBHW060110260726
48658CB00004B/1482

9 798879 360158